PAPER

POEMS OF SHIN DAL-JA

TRANSLATED BY CHO YOUNG-SHIL

FORSYTHIA

2018

AN IMPRINT OF CODHILL PRESS

FORSYTHIA

an imprint of

CODHILL PRESS

Codhill books are published by David Appelbaum for Codhill Press

PAPER

Support for the publication of this work has been generously provided by the Daesan Foundation, and acknowledged with gratitude.

Book Design by Jana Potashnik
BAIRDesign, Inc. · bairdesign.com

ISBN-13: 978-1-930337-96-1
ISBN-10: 1-930337-96-5

Printed in the United States of America

FOR ALL WHO ARE IN LOVE WITH PAPER

CONTENTS

THE AUTHOR'S NOTE

THE FIRST GLIMMER OF AN IDEA for a book of paper poems came to me a long time ago. Seven years have gone by already. I kept postponing the job. There were reluctant doubts whether the idea will indeed make poetry. Some 100 poems dwindled to fewer and fewer as I continued to expunge more and more.

Then the voice saying paper is on rapid decline grew louder and louder. Some even stated that paper is now defunct. I was pressed hard. Commensurate with the comfort civilization has given me, the mind has yet become bleak. I wanted to bring man's good nature and beauty in concert with the thing called paper. Warmth, eternity, spiritual labor, fullness, conciliation, peace, love, motherhood, purity, home, naiveté—I wanted to unite all the emotional stuff that irrefutably commingle into a single element, and portray it as 'paper.'

It was shocking to hear the news that they are preparing a seed storage near polar icecaps, where icebergs are now thawing. The seeds vanishing because of environmental ravage may signify mutual destruction of men and natural environment. Hence, the seed copyright—a fairly new term to our ears—vouching the future for flowers and fruits and trees, will actually bring about men's survival as well.

This poetry book is a grain of seed in light of my longing for warm human nature, and of my effort to restore it; it also bears a poet's love for paper.

OPENING POEM

Rife are the rumors
So paper will be a thing of the past?

I therefore went to an empty field,
carefully spread open one page of stillness
  consoling the forlorn field after harvest
Then to a trail in the woods I went, where
leaves were murmuring softly,
  birds deftly composing lyrics to their
own songs for a small concert
Now to a graceful Korean-style house's
courtyard I've come, awaiting on my feet
  one great script by the stroke of the fish
in motion, here in this small pond

what could replace the paper?

You will be sorely missed
Paper is man's mind
called a faultless god much revered,
what then shall a poet write on it?

THE SOUL OF ART

A pen
reaches for the paper

The paper
with its heart's throbbing pulse
receives
the tip of the pen

At the nadir of the paper
bestirs
the soul of art bearing an artisan's fine craft

A splendid task
to dredge up words
mute with a thousand sealed mouths
An immutable heritage
from God to man

The very instant
a man's heart touches the paper's heart

it so galvanizes his mind
even the chaos of human folly rights itself bolt upright.

CHARM

Dear Child,
If you're getting on the internet
take with you
a sheet of paper, just like a charm
If you pass through fleshpots
where temptations are rampant,
or get snatched by the ankle
by those genome genes,
or lose sight in the web of radio waves
flashing in torrents,
or face
monsters, bogs, fierce winds,
then listen to the paper's voice
rising clear and crisp

If you tire out, all giddy
flustered navigating
from site to site,
then take a sheet of blank paper
and with all your mind
write down each letter of your name
stroke by stroke.

THE SOUND OF A BELL

Do you hear a bell ringing inside the paper?

A bell ringing
the instant you give up the passion of desires
in front of the paper
with nothing to see
nothing to hear

Heavy shoulders drooping
you've walked past the din twirling like rags
around the ears
through the forest of buildings rising like rage,
where flashing lights look daggers
still more at sundown,
then you face the paper in earnest;

the instant you rub hands together
so your warm human breath thaws
the word 'purity' wrapped in clear plastic and frozen

a bell coming on crystal-clear from the dark
subterranean deep
and ringing in my heart

The bell is ringing.

PERILOUS POLE

A pageful of darkness flips over
In the meantime
the letters trickling over this day's page
trickle down anew,
men who swore to guard themselves intact slip
and tumble down,
glorious rosy civilizations surge and surge
filling up every nook and cranny
finally to drive them out to a perilous pole to dwell,
those who distort life jostle toward it;
maybe a swine's passing through
maybe a starved wolf's passing through
listless, headless men tumbling down....

PAPER COMFORTER

Here's a scene—a form huddled up on the cement ground
shivering with ague
as if this fitful fever was yet a sign of life
His frazzled flesh, in truth,
sheeting the moaning ground
A disregarded, dubious, obscure mark
lying down in the wintry subway passage,
a sheet of paper sheltering him from the world's winds
a sheet of paper holding all of his past years
His hearing impaired long ago, but
perhaps well acquainted with the bitter winds
sweeping up from below
perhaps knowing a hand in this, giving him a good wave, pulling his frost-bitten ear,
he now curls in his toes, remembering the warmth
from the sheet of paper
Where to go now,
the man, slowly inclining his head in the direction
of his soul's destination,
opens his mouth, looking dead yet not stone-dead, then shuts it
Vested with a sheet of paper the man crossing
the abysmal heart of winter.

LIBRARY

Should we guard you hand in hand?

And console you

with our dances beneath the full moon?

Oh tower

of the mind!

We're sorry, ailing paper,

had there been some misunderstanding that you're on the wane

From your moaning

I shall draw moonlight to moisten my lips with.

RADIANCE

How radiant—
that shade so soft and elegant
One close look upon the exquisite magnolia petals,
one may go blind
Never have I seen such paper
A ray of wisdom born of flower petals
quietly saying,
Distill and write, O poets, write down
the world's meaning veiled in mystery
and its beauty
Eyes shut tight, I am enthralled
I too want to forge, and bury in such paper a single
line of my life's poem
Not knowing what those poets of magnolia hue
will write
magnolias bloom again
this spring.

BREAST

Is there milk in the paper, I wonder
Two large breasts
Mother's milk
with which to raise fools and cowards

Between my breasts full and high
and Mother's saggy and flabby
between my daughter's breasts firm and full
and mine now flat as flat can be

is there in the paper the name Mother
the great holder of life
the very breast
raising vast acres of dreams

of thoughts, of creations, of future?

HAND PRINTING

Out I thrust both hands
Are you confident?
Is it fine to expose all the
fingerprints of the sand-
blown desert
whose whirlwind
whirling round your
neck left all these rings?
No smoothness here
How jagged, there's no
sense of stability as if
whipped by wind's keen
blade
I may have to regret this
sorely
Having laid down my
hands, apart from me,
I feel uneasy and pitiful
Suddenly towering in my
face is the plight
of the woman who's been
walking over gravel on
her hands, feet up
in the air

This may well be called
your own heart that has
spilled out
Yours after all, but
don't they seem too
foreign?
Compressed flat here
is
the brutal history
of an aged servant
who's shed her mask,
spewed out all vanity,
to the last speck
Is it fine to copy
these hands— not to
be varnished again
anyhow—
and nail it down like a
thing of disgrace in the
eye of God?

BLANK PAPER 1

If you wish to quell your adamantine fury
and bear your stony grief
then try to enter that place
If you wish to open your mind to virgin nature
where, no matter how far you go, there's no end in sight
but the vast expanse without floor or wall
If you wish to steal into blank paper
and be one with it and taste the bliss
If you wish to be cleansed of the world's impurity
and be as pure as sylvan spring
If you wish to enter a good path
where your first step will set you in eternity
—a white light with terrible depths
receiving and repelling all things—
and your next open the path to past and future
If you wish to meet with the Mind of all minds with
no weight, no odor, no collision

One such path wherein you have nothing yet possess
all things
one such wellhead that leads you step by step:
there the heart is reassured wherever you follow
unblemished hearts stand tall and erect
wise convictions command
and you will never thirst no matter how far you venture....

MOTHER SAID, YOUR FIRST FLOWERS

As a young girl
I once felt like a bit of soft flesh fall off my crotch
Mother said
You see, it's your first flowers
I thought hard but it didn't seem like flowers
so I locked the door, dabbed the thing on the paper;
was no flesh, nor red blood,
nor anything like flowers
A fatal memorandum
portending the foray of the one
who offered up to paper her first menstruation
her virginity
and thus had intimacy with the paper,
from whence she will not part ever.

DARK GREEN PAPER

I keep writing, but see no letters: Summer leaves are
too dark in color scheme

All day long birds wiggle their miniscule foot-brushes
to write something; passing winds
  ask whatever it is they're writing

Go away, Birdheads, scrawls the rain's thick brushes
streaking down from the sky; clouds just cock their
heads bewildered

A brush will not write where it's too dark
The darkness in these leaves is too deep.

PAPER MULBERRY

I'd love to write on that leaf, 'Paper'

At the entrance of the Samsung Press Museum
by Gugi-Tunnel, Seoul, stands a paper mulberry
Today at the museum's dedication ceremony, I for the first time see the tree
said to have been planted by Mr. Lee Uh-Ryong,
yet I find it quite familiar
Hundreds of truckloads of paper that have come to me
may well have originated in that tree
Should I be talking to that one leaf
one hundred years will swiftly fly away.

DESERT

A message came from the desert
Inscribed there were camels' hoofprints
I tore open the desert
and brought it to light
With a whoosh sandy winds gushed forth
cabling in letters the paper's soul.

TILLING OF THE MIND

Paper… Do not rush to lay hands on it

Once inside, there's an infinite stretch of barren soil
Put your whole life to plow it
you still cannot till even a single parcel

A hoe, a pick, a shovel,
or whatever farm tool you may plow with
you won't be able to cull a single word silver-pure as
an eye

Why not plow with your heart!
To call a scar a flower is
an oxymoron,
whose midair steps you mount and mount
and mount again, you still cannot reach
Yes, indeed,
why not tear your living eyes out
and light them.

SALT

One sets fire
It flames up
A mere sheet of paper
burning out in fleeting seconds
There silently fritters
the paper's death
Upon it rise up like a castle
printed words come back to life
Man's abode
that cannot be burned down
The white mind
sparkles as a few grains of salt
taking away earthly impurity.

SNOWSTORM

Earthly paper is
so much too black
for a poet to sing

There's one who looks upon
a poet weeping
holding on to pitch-black paper

and the heavens
pour down
paper after paper white and pure silver
upon the black village of poets

A snowstorm it is.

FOOTPRINTS

Who has walked this way?
Trailing along carefully, piously
opening up each footprint
for a perusal
I find a copy of an autobiography
set down in a stormy gush
Is this someone I know well?
A cliff at end of a long lane, a
hoarse voice, and numb hands
Putting my own over a footprint
I try to read still deeper breath
even, then
who can this be?
I return to the first page and leaf
through, eyes wide open;
Yes, yes, this all-night-long
March snowstorm out of season
is for a good perusal once more.

KOREAN PAPER

How did you like the
feel of space?

Past sunlight, past
thunder cracking
bloody, past storms
beating wild

then past the pallid
moonlight, past spring
breeze soft as fresh
mugwort

finally beaten again
and again into the
Korean paper

The paper's resilient
spirit has defeated
death

A sprout rising out of
wintry earth

that has embraced all
things world spews out

and is now going
frozen slow-paced

in deep silence

Soundless

the majestic human
spirit is born here.

GRAFFITI

That jumbled writing, and clumsy drawing of a train
I never saw
on the walls of my childhood home
In that lonely room of my heart that knew not where
else to unload its load
my crippled writing could never straighten itself
the blurred train never once moved on its own
So slow were they that my mind arose first
and hurried to Seoul, and now and then
my graffiti beats its broken wings in my heart
Underneath the flutter faster than my pulse
sprouts an immaculate seed rice of imagination
Pristine spirit
the very wellspring of Art was in it.

THIN ICE

Thin ice…
Is the word 'thin ice' someone's
hand or what, it keeps touching me
I can see so well myself, twenty and
shiny crystalline
Flesh so soft, that hand keeps
rubbing my own flesh: a glimpse
of that flesh
still smarting
just about to shatter; would that
the glass paper
ever so gently cut me, and I shed
drops of red blood, a sad gash—
so at twenty, down in my heart
I swore, with a cut on my lip,
to strive against a sheet of paper
I will immerse myself in the paper's
soul as if crossing a paper bridge,
this thin-iced road
I will have my lip cut yet again.

HUMAN SKIN

Do you know that there's this human skin?
That they made books out of men's skin?
Well, history tells Europeans also made
books out of white men's skin
In 16th century Netherlands, I hear,
they excoriated slaves, prisoners, or
corpses
to get paper for making books
It's reported the leather of 0.41 millimeter
human skin made
books soft to the touch, easy to turn,

which means that men had words to leave
behind, even by such brutal means
Their desire, fiercer than an animal's,
drove them to action
It's told some old libraries covertly keep
a few books made out of human skin;

should paper disappear
and get more scarce than modern
technology itself...
will we be hearing of the rape of men's skin
rather than of sexual violence often
reported lately?

THE GREAT UNIVERSE

A lifetime of seven decades
I put in paper
Put all of the four seasons
as you see
Recorded in minute detail
America, France, and Asia
in accordance with the tide of 21st Century
Wove in rich tapestry
sympathy, humiliation, enrapture
and betrayal, that throws you down and out,
of those people I've met over six decades
for one's life requires signs of others
My tears turned from white to dense gray
then from dew-glistening green
to red as heart, and all these I lick and survive
having long since stripped myself of ancient solitude
Took my lover's soul, threw it in unreserved,
an act that will raise not so small a ruckus if discovered
Even slipped in the unknown future
futile as it is
And of course, heaped so high the invisible God's Word
that it flowed on end

How absurd
I haven't even filled the bottom
of this one sheet of paper yet.

FIGURATION

Figuratively
a million birds entered
it. No trace. Still thin.
Figuratively
a million tons of
rocks rolled into it.
Vanished. Still thin.
Figuratively
fishes, thrashing and
dragging the sea, swam
into it. All lay there.
Still thin.
Figuratively
all of the villagers were
swept away, sucked
into it. All quiet. Still
thin.
Figuratively
in the quiet utterly
thin, utterly dry

figuratively
telling me to revive the
sounds of those birds,
rocks, fishes, human
beings
to tear at their cries
with my teeth,
its gun of awareness
leveled at me, eyes
wide open,
this sheet of paper.

DEATH PENALTY BY POISON

Takes capital punishment by poison

Takes another capital punishment by poison

Drinks up more poison for a millionth capital
punishment

He

never once has died

So fierce

the mind of the paper

sparkles even in the face of men's apostasy.

PUPPY LOVE

I saw the lad of my puppy
love I had met at thirteen

Saw the young puppy
love, now in his seventies

Saw the puppy love of my
shy, youthful days

Still in pink

is the young puppy love,
now thin-haired and
bald-headed

The days of our life

soaked in

like a sheet of spotless
paper.

ANALOGUE

Press the secret code, then swing opens
the ultramodern gate
That's unpolished, now just a touch of
your fingerprint slides open
the upscale gate, with a *Yes, yes, yes*
That's bothersome, just say *It's me,*
your voice now opens
the gate as regal as can be
Very soon, for sure
all you have to do is stand at the door
and the instant it scents you the owner
it'll click open

But I like slow things
A warm door someone rushes to and
opens with a smile
welcoming you with a mortal voice and
mortal hands
when your weary hand presses the bell;
if not that
some fond brushwood door at a kin's
on your mother's side,
that comes down only to your knees,
left open night and day.

THE AMISH

I've seen a heavenly book on earth.
Heard one Word engraved on earth,
sweet and clean as a newborn's heart.
The Amish who inhabit Lancaster County,
Pennsylvania, America.
New leaves born of heavens are the Amish,
who live a natural life
in a nature free of automobiles, electricity,
piped water or schools.
Nature's farmers who, renouncing civilization,
lead a life without civilization as did
  Jesus.
Nature's masters in compliance with nature,
they are pregnant with nature, engender
  nature. Unsullied are they.
The people registering fresh fruits on a clean
plate. In the village with no power line,
they take all the sun and star lights to plant the
whole sky in their bosom. And for lack
of petty pleasure, beget child after child.

Nature's father, nature's sons, they seem like a
sheet of God's clean paper.
Atop the roof in the street, where not cars but
stagecoaches come and go in state, perches
sunlight shining as if laving. In silence I walked
on for the heaven I sought was
right there; my body grew so light, nearly
translucent, I soared up and up;
couldn't even put a period, everything turning
translucent on that pristine, vivid paper
I didn't bring back even a single sheet of it,
I left all behind;
left all my footprints even....

WIND POEM

Wind built a house
Built it inside a radish

Wish I could enter
the white flesh so deep and sheltered
in the dead of winter

Wind too
was in need of a house of white flesh
longing for a sure retreat
as it bent low
and burrowed into the radish?
In need of the paper's quiet secret?

MEN-EATING WOMAN

That bitch! She's messed up so many, but still
hungry, goes panting whenever a guy shows up,
I tell yer
At *Jujube*, a bar at the humble foothill of
Wontong-ri, Namwon, in Cholla Province
the hostess was heaping acrimonious insults
on
the lass still tender-cheeked
Who knows the full story
but, just one look at her body, you can tell
unnumbered men have eaten her up; a sudden,
cold shiver
runs along my arms; who's going to loose her
from this heavy implacable breathing?
The hostess showers curses on her to keep her
from running away, but blood is up
in the latter's silent eyes; world staggers...
One whole page of that young thing's heart's
been ripped apart, now blown in wind,
I tell yer....

GROWING PAIN

Even on the rice in the
brass bowl I wrote, and
heard a sound
Wrote on the sawdust
in the village lumber
too, and ate the sound
Wrote on the snow
fallen white
on the dirt playground
on the sand by the
stream as well, and
gave wings to the
sound
Wrote on the water in
the wash basin too
The sound developed
fins
I told myself no one
should see this
I even wrote in haste
a lad's name; Crape
myrtle bloomed way
before the season
Wrote on the wind
sweeping ahead,
perhaps did too deep,
the air retained my
writing
The sound penetrated
the air
The remains of my
older brother killed in
the Korean War,
on his warm ashes too
I wrote
and my fingertips,
tingling, went numb
How much more to
write to be filled up?
The tale of the
schooling of a pure-
hearted but slow-
witted country girl,
who
adopted as her
notebook even the
twenty-year-old
brother's grave the size
of a herb
basket.

HIPS

The lead of my pencil broke helplessly
At every writing
the paper ripped easily
for its quality was uneven
What I missed was softness

One day at daybreak
the floor was all moonlight
and Mother was sitting on the
chamber pot, her hips bared
I wished to catch that water, a shower
pouring straight down
unlikely to shatter,
and write on those hips large
quite white and fleshy
a vow in one line, drenched in
moonlight
I wished to write one line of my
anguished love letter.

A SACRED PLACE

A snowflake caresses the sloping back of the Himalaya
Is it there yet?
A spiderling is tugging at a pigtail of the universe
Is it there yet?
Let's say a woodpecker pecked the earth's brow to a
red flower
Is it there yet?
If we beat down all untruth and violence
could we set forth on that distant path?

If we fall prostrate

on our faces

flat on the ground

our mouths sealed, ears open

then ears closed, eyes open

to creep

toward one perfected pen stroke

our eyes closed, navel unclosed?

THE WAVE

Who has so carelessly wrinkled up the blue paper?

Wrinkled yet musical, I would say

That one vital current

lending your veins tremulous

as by the pitch of your arm

you crumple up a page of your life

gone awry day to day

and fling it into a trash can;

its ultimate force

spurring you to rise up

yet again.

PAPER BOOK

Though pressed to
please step back

Though needled much
like an illicit child

Though kindly nudged
to turn and be gone

Though sneered to
be, say, a pad for the
e-book rather

it just stands tall
keeping the same
form, the same place

How commanding

In nature
easy: It rips, wears,
blanches, its letters
wax faint,
is palpable and
so precious that

one earmarks for
rereading;
one places it on his
bosom when drowsy,
or pillows his head on
a couple of them

It resembles the scale
fabric the scholars
of Chosun Dynasty
draped themselves
with
  against cold

and has the force of a
grindstone

grinding the mind's
blade

forever

by spending itself.

TRUTH, TERRORIST

Did the blue-black wind, wheezing up
the hilltop, drop them off one after
another on
 the pass while briefly gathering breath?

They are nowhere to be found

Those faceless armed thugs who even
slash off women's breasts

The living thing in one's bottom, lit into
black fires, also flickers away

The paintings on the naked bodies,
whipped up with bottomless passion,

are now gone as is their youth;

once

a fiery arrow,

one's quick brush ply by ply went away
also without a goodbye.

KELP PAPER

Maybe we've bent on animalism too much
Too animalistic, the world
has been panting and gasping
Starving, we've been gorging ourselves
At this time as we are cloyed and our hearts turn into
empty fields
so our greed is heavier than our bodies
and even the paper pours forth muck

they say kelp paper's just round the corner
Parading the placard reading Biodegradable
kelp paper of chaste vegetable property is about to be born
Kelp paper
of the body of seaweed ten million times acquainted with
briny breath
ten million times tossed and inured by breakers
the soul of the sea added thereto

Like a voice of my heart barely throbbing in this age
when, as they say, the pulse of poetry lives and thrives,
like the blue voice of the sea
kelp paper is about to....

MAGNUM OPUS

Do not say that from dawn to dusk you
plodded upon darkness

Nor that all night long you ascended and
descended Yochul Valley in Mt. Deokyu

Nor that you roved, your whole body
beating and stomping darkness harder
than granite,

walked through steely darkness, and
were bloodied

Nor that your sinking spirit was like a
leaf on a foothill, weather-worn and
crushed

This dazzle life full of limber tears
welling up in the terror of total privation

Do not let your mouth tell

what immortal thing both your feet
wrote down in the dark.

TRUNDLE THE HEART

I played with mother's tears
Played at soaps
As bubbles began rising up Mother gasped heavier
I puffed tears, floated them up, plenty of them
Fed rose moss, marvel-of-Peru, balsam, each a drop
of tear Mother shed last night
They laughed better
I too chortled along
Laughing arrested, I trundled the loop of a teardrop
In the courtyard radiant with morning sunlight in full
smile after the dark
the most beautiful rainbow in the world was wheeling
Is it a filial, or prodigal heart to trundle round and
round
an angular fringe of mother's hard life?
With mother's tears I made a beanbag
A beanbag made of her white sock I stole and stuffed
with her tears

I made a whole lot of errors pitching and
catching it, which was more like her innards
Played toss-and-catch with my mother's tears
Tossed up her tears but what I caught in my
hand was a piece of red flesh
Oh this is fun, I trundled the loop again,
now two drops of tears, then ten,
I trampled upon the deaths of tears
The very instant Mother drew her last breath
under my feet
what I was holding in my hand was her heart.

BLANK PAPER 2

Cut the gullet
deplume and
gut it
clean it in water, then place on a white plate
there you have a whole raw chicken
Oh no!
For a spell I was looking for something to write with.

CALL 911

It's way too simple
Just click, no sweat
So simple
you get on easy and get off broken
When you get on the computer
words break up first
No human words but some goblin's?
Troll, ALOL , WTH, wOOt, 21, 411, WAA...
Maybe we morph into animals or space men
while on it,
the linguistic evolution in this age
of new-minted words?
Too busy; No time; Cut your sentences short
Why write words!
Is there a magic wind blowing in it?
Are there quick teeth in it, gnawing human
heart and brain
and his eternal substance?
Hands up!
That which collapses is
after all our mind
Call 911.

FLASHING ON ME

As a freshman
philosophy book in my hands
I took on my shoulders the whole of human anguish:
philosophy, or poetry?
Eager for a nocturnal glimpse of Seoul, reluctant to go
to sleep,
I strolled Hyochang Park at the crack of dawn;
the dawn of Seoul rose in deep blue
and suddenly a stave flashed on me
only to fly away on my way home;
no stubby pencil, no scrap, in my pocket,
in a flurry I plucked a twig
and wrote down my line bold
under a magnolia tree
then raced home, grabbed a pencil and paper,
raced back as if to save a life;
but under no tree
was my poem to be found, all gone
my brain too robbed clean,
who on earth ran away with it;
that great line I haven't retrieved yet
and wandering, uneasy spell, desperate waiting,
insomnia
have been my chronic illness ever since;
even the hieroglyphic scribbled with bloody fingernail
on the back of my hand
can't bring back the one great line of that time.

FURROW

That deep canyon,
I'd love to erect a Buddhist temple there
Those waves
in the wake of your life's track
watchfully trodden, without being glum,
their motions are now stilled in the depths;
gracious are you
I'd love to lie down in the bed of that
comfortable silence
The flow
formed deep where you surrendered
everything
did not drift away in the wind
That face so furrowed
as if the rice-sheaves of her life farmed
all through life
are stacked thereon
The brilliant
pattern glimpsed over time
as if bearing in it rapture and solace
Look closely, they are not just slough.

POND

Whose signature could
this be—
In Yulmae, a village
in Sancheong in the
Southern Gyungsang
Province,
a good distance from
Mt. Jiri,
there's a round pond
that never dries for a
thousand years

All of Mt. Jiri into one
paper scroll
outcry upon outcry
that masterpiece some
two feet fashioned
at every bend, at end of
whose labor
I imagine a stamp
burnished in grave
bitterness
was set in signature
here;
the flame's glorious
mutation in this
unforgettable moment
Where have I seen a
well's signature
bearing the nakedness
of winds and shy
clouds of yore?
In Yulmae, Sancheong,
way down Mt. Jiri,
a village the sky nudges
clouds for a visit,
there's a pond
a red signature
made when the
Chonwang Peak bent
over, stamped with his
brow,
all those beautiful
azalea blossoms
reflected red in it.

PAPER BOAT

There was no bigger boat
than that
With tiny hands perhaps
the size of newly sprung
shoots
I used to make boats
out of paper scraps from
mother's Korean jacket
pattern
and from my elder
sister's paper cranes,
out of that paper more
precious than money
Just as my big sister
made a hundred paper
cranes wishing for a
woman's hopes
I too made a hundred
paper boats and floated a
woman's dreams
A long way for a hundred
dreams, but
every night I floated
them off lovingly
Every night I sent them
to an unknown land
Every night I floated
my paper boats to
somewhere I should be
I always lived in the
unknown

My future, my love,
my dreams, my
imagination, were my
paper boats' constant
cargo Those paper
boats I've launched all
through my life—were
they having smooth
sails?
Crawling up the steep
slope of my life, I could
tell that after departing
from me my paper
boats had it rough; Did
my paper boat pass
over my life, when I
surrendered myself,
prostrate with both
hands up?

FATHER

One could call it a fatal bankruptcy, irrevocable
abandonment
When he just turned sixty my father was a wreck,
all his youth and wealth and honor completely
wrecked
A man who loved women, loved songs, and loved
*padduk**
And a moment came when his gamesmanship failed
him
The stones began falling off the board,
women fled off, youth died away, honor was lost,

songs ceased, his mighty virility wilted
There was a son who wished to disown his paternal
blood even
Father hid himself behind 50 volumes of diary
Living but dead, dead but living—waxed pallid, he
withdrew himself into the house of
  paper
Began to rise from the stark bottom to be a father with
a new name, a true self, a real
  man, and a new life

Empty hands at home with his paper...unadorned and
subdued, he was reborn as a fresh
  essence, no more aloneness
His eyes opened; till now blinded by sumptuous
wealth, ostensible fame,
  and vile capacity for padduk, but now they opened:
the eye gained after all was lost
Father drew his last breath in his diary, passed into an
honest essence.

* It is a Korean equivalent of European chess.

COUGHING UP BLOOD

Our tile-roofed palatial house fell into another's hands
and Mother popped in her mouth 30 sleeping pills, an attempt at suicide
Why have you brought me back? She howled with rage, but then gathered herself;
Shame, shame on us, at two in the morning we shot the moon
to a suburb of Seoul a twelve-hour drive by truck
As if dumb she kept mum for three months, closed her ear for three months,
just sat against the wall, like a tree or stone,
then she wailed a long while, longer than a forest fire red-flaming
Her despair singed into ashes
Her bloody wailing ceasing
she held a pencil as she would a dagger,
begged for a piece of paper
practiced with bloody zeal the illiterate's elemental ka na da

then three years later came a single
letter to this daughter:
"Dont foget what I say, Study til you
die, Make monney,
Dont live like me, Be happey"
A bloody lump poured on that paper
A last will breathing in the paper now
in frame,
still warm and lumpy.

PAPER ROAD

The Egyptians wrote on papyrus.
Papyrus leaves were unmanageable like inhibited women, vulnerable like feeble women.
In the region of Mesopotamia, I read, they made cuneiform characters by pressing
coarse reed stalks on the clay, too heavy for both famished arms and massive as boulder.
A laborious toil.
In India or Eastern Asia they wrote on leaves, in China on bamboo strips or wood pieces. They had to hold letters as dear as their own blood.
Sometimes silk was used, though too pricey. People simply couldn't pour forth all the
words teeming in their breast. There was a fire in them. They were itching to give
utterances.
In place of paper, they even made parchment out of thin layer of sheepskin. Man's
hunger for recorded civilization resulted in countless animals' death.
Therewith, therefore, nonetheless,
human race invented paper.

Some say Chae Ryun, the Han Dynasty Chinese,
invented paper, but I reckon that even
before him a wish to record and an appetence to write
made paper in sleepless
nights.
A breathing man must have been driven wild by a
mortal urge not only to eat but to write.
What can it be but that fierce urge that launched
civilization.
However, Chae Ryun, entangled in a Court plot, was
executed by being poisoned
and Go Sunji the hero of the Battle of Talas who gave
the Arab world knowledge of
paper, and Abbasid Caliph, were killed by political
enemies.
After many a hero's death and Pharaoh's curses the
paper stands before us.
Bow to the paper.
The paper too marched the selfsame road Genghis
Kahn marched to attack, only mightier.
It is the Paper Road. The road for the soul.

THE HUMAN BUTTERFLY

"First throw me down before cutting the tree down."

On the northern California coast there's a forest awash with sky-high redwoods, where the 'Human Butterfly' lives. Her name: Julia Butterfly Hill (24 at the time.) She's protesting against the felling scheduled by a lumber company, a human shield for a tree. She climbed into Luna, a redwood as tall as a 20-story building, and hasn't come down over a year. Single-handedly running the hazards of storms and showers and lumber company, she manifested a fiery will declaring that she'd come down only if they promise to preserve the forest.

The Hill who communicates with the world through her solar cell phone, and continues campaigning to change the world. By means of a burner she makes simple meals out of foodstuff pulled up by rope, takes showers in rainwater, writes letters on leaves up there, electronically gives lectures on the importance of a forest, draws pictures or crafts poems.

She writes of the blessed nature, of beautiful forest, and of our freedom to be happy therein.

Hill's poems are alive with the purpose of protecting these. I was about to say they are beautiful, but refrain myself. Forceful rather than beautiful.

When asked if she wasn't scared, she replied, Yes, scared, but I'd be more scared if the forest dies. The first time she saw the redwood forest she was moved to tears. How frustrating that a forest with such great beauty should be felled down. Her own youthfulness and a certain impetus led her to climb up there. And she fought. And won the world to her side. Those who cherished hope worldwide applauded her, for they care for living things.

Necessities and encouragements were delivered to the redwood forest. People wanted to share courage even from the ground. Julia Butterfly Hill, you are Woman of all women. A heroine at 24. And a poet who saves the earth.

"Trees are not our money source but our life; they'll become paper that saves lives!"

This is the poet who pens her poems by the might of her will.

* The Headwater Forest in California, the last of the habitats for redwoods, is one of the spots where environmental preservation activism forcefully breaks forth. An activist fighting for the cause there over ten years even lost his life. The tree that Hill the Human Butterfly ascended was over one thousand years old, worth at least ten thousand dollars. After successfully preventing the felling of the tree she continued her fight, maintaining that the authorities were slack in taking appropriate measure for the Forest, and then descended the tree about two years later.

FAN

A mountain unfolds
Sounds of clear water, the Gaya harp
playing in every valley deep*
Even if you sit in the hallway
it's like facing the summit

The wind lying in the mountain shade
came racing swiftly
upon hearing its own name called

Recollected as wind—but
it is a pure spirit coming near:

a deep sound rustling against bamboo
leaves
a murmur of the Korean paper below its
breath

A universe folds, then
another unfolds.

* The Gaya harp is a twelve-stringed Korean harp.

STELLAR

One summer midnight
I was lying on a flat bench
counting stars in the sky;
the smudge fire by my flank
stung my eyes
but I still would ascend into the
starry sky
borne upon a wisp of the smoke
Just lift hands, gathering a few
stars was that easy
With them I played house
Star salad
Rice named Star
Even fixed a meat dish named Star
and called myself Stellar
Stellar paper I am; an artisan
crafting with stellar paper
setting a stellar table, inscribing
on the star its name
But I know outside the window
there's a terror
named Civilization, whipping up
that innocent daughter's skirt.

ISLAND

Do not enter! Seagulls,
perhaps the district leaders,
rifle the motor boat that
transports
  people, busy warding
off virus in their rushed
language, mew, keow, ha-
ha-ha-ha
Eyes goggling, suspecting
the land is infested with
germs, the birds watch the
incomers;
 who knows if they're saying
we folks may disembark or
may not, I myself can't
 decipher their passwords
but one thing's clear: You
mustn't spill germs here.
Like paper, the island is the
last
  comfort for the broken-
hearted; I think I can
understand this much.

GOURD

In the temple well in a
recess of a mountain
I dip the gourd and
have a drink of water
Living trees, vigilant
stars
Having had a drink of
water
streaming from time
immemorial
I am revived
So this is a gourd
They brought down
the round moon afloat
over thatched roof,
emptied out the inside
that resembles cooked
white rice
and made a nature's
bowl of it for use

With a gourd beggars
begged for food
and when cracked
mother's mother with
her needle sewed it up
to carry on with life
again
They all seemed
poverty-stricken yet
mild.

SKIRT

The trailing skirt of a *kisaeng of old
was the most extravagant of all kinds of paper
Blustery, bearded men with intense gaze swooped down upon her
and when he picked a skirt and wrote a line of poetry
the ink seeped down the woman's entire body
even through her bone marrows;
she learned by heart those fingertips
and holding the hem of her skirt to her bosom,
recalled the shared sentiment:
so, from lips to breast to waist, then go below the waist, then where...
The life of a skirt ever spinning round and round in the same spot.

* They were talented artists who entertained wealthy men, or government officials.

THE SUBWAY

You know that there's a
rail under my heart,
that a guy with ever
subtle ways is running,
that he runs and runs
floundering in the dark
but will never reach the
destination
A guy who thus cannot
stop running
You know that you're
running through the
dark underground
running through the
path in my bone
scraped out in my
breast

Desiring to leave with
me just one word
and surely burnish just
one line into my body
you burrowed your
way into my bones and
entered
A guy who runs along
the rail he scraped out
under my heart
because nowhere in
the world can we stand
side by side
You who pass through
my bones again today
shrieking with high-
voltage, abrasive
metallic noise,
screech,
because now out of this
world you can't say a
word.

AUTUMN FIELD

Look upon the autumn field
after they sow and reap three thousand times,
then sow and reap another three thousand
The still of one leaf of paper grown immensely
sensitive
Even the wind sails on modestly, attired neatly
In truth, liberal mind and broad bosom with
profound, patient endurance
When a proud winged creature happens to
drop droppings in its flight
this paper sops it up, just as writing paper
would ink water
What a charitable paper
The young moon who intended to pass over
quietly finds it cannot
even take one step—despite such welcome—
and halts trembling.

SOONCHON BAY

Is your vision gradually
getting blurry?
Let us go to Soonchon Bay
Is your certain body part
gradually hardening like
limestone?
Let us go to Soonchon Bay
Spitting out sticky black
blood?
Let us go to Soonchon Bay
Let us go and see what
living things there are
When you go past the Bay's
Sanctuary to the mudflat
and see a family of black
cranes, let us ask them why
they live there
When you see whooper
swans, yellow-billed
herons, or black-headed
gulls
ask them why they
winter there, against
the lure of warm cities;
the reeds with their
slender bodies
huddled together
against the cold,
let us ask them as they
lean on each other with
their dry bones
as if to share warmth,
withholding dry
coughs
Let us incline our ears
to that marsh
stretching out its black
limbs, setting itself as
dense as can be
Pristine life breathing,
coming closer
in thunderous
stillness....

BLANK PAPER 3

First, all saltiness had to be removed
The time spent to dry a single teardrop— I'd scoop
up one whole sea the same way, drop
  by drop
A century ebbed away slowly
While another century was wearing on I dried wet
hours
Next came the elaborate formal work, drawing all
the blood
You see that the paper also has desires? The
moment blood is drawn to the last drop, the very
 blood that ploughs desires as sod, there blossoms
whitely a stretch of desert
Over that
desert is a poet who's plodding, hobbling.

LUMP

A heart's fruit, or a grown-up's secret tube?
It was a village market day: As I hunkered
down half a day in front of our mill leading to
the market, men and ladies each with a lump
on their faces proudly walked by
I wished to take a lump larger than my ten-
year old dream
and blow into a balloon

Could it be that Civilization was hollow?
All those secret codes it gulped down
hide in the stomach, in the large intestine
and pancreas, in the womb and breasts
to finally devour men;
I miss that lump bulging on the shoulder of a
woman selling rice-cake.

NOBODY HERE

A few lines of blurred scribbling erased clean
not a bird winging through
totally blank
is this sheet of paper

In a room, on the floor, in the street, in a movie
theater, in a café
at the train station, at the airport, in the sea or
mountain or river or a snack bar

I am alone

I erase the word 'alone'

then myself

Released and
refreshed am I.

PAPER PORRIDGE

Have you ever eaten paper porridge?

The sea and river
the sky and sea
conciliation and peace
purity and true human nature kneaded altogether
and boiled at 1000 degrees in a crucible,
have you ever drunk a glass of serenity so made?

Remove from the world's proverbs any imperfection
let your spiritual silence and contemplation
be so very pure
exercise patience abiding
and let a balmy Word be born
O world!
I will apply it to your sore
I will serve you a bowlful of paper porridge
in a vessel named Mind.

JORGES LUIS BORGES

A book, a country, came into the world

On August 24, 1899
lightning flashed through
Grandfather's library, shaking heaven
and earth
and a book came into the world
In the library his shoulders and thighs
grew thick
smell of paper, scent of books, set his
veins quivering
Page by page, the letters were stored in
his respiratory organs
to nurture him with the knowledge
from the East and the West
Paper's lifeblood, books' ideas, began
circulating in his body
A book living among books
erecting a castle of books
serving as a librarian
then as the curator of the National
Library
being a book himself, all his life:

Jorges Luis Borges

What bookworm dared do that?
In the end he lost sight, read by the books' scent
tunneled through darkness, navigated letters beyond
darkness
pored over the Braille text running his fingers over it
attained clearer understanding of letters
and that infinity became fragrance for his life
Ever so deep, the sea of his consciousness
was indeed a castle of books, higher than the Great
Wall of China
On June 14, 1986 his mind's eyes sealed up forever
His books are but still growing copious.

SCENT

At end of mire comes a flower

One hundred years from mire to flower

At end of silence

all scentless, comes a voice

One thousand years from silence to voice

Lips sealed and body closed

not a sound spilling out

she is flung onto a miry road

Therefore

lips sealed again, only persisting

Flower fostered fragrance within, walking the mire
still

The scent of Chinese ink permeating into the paper.

DEATH

The throat so swollen, I guess there will be no more talking

The earth shaking all over, the roaring quake

charges human bodies with reeking stenches

rankling into hopeless symptoms of the end stage

Could it at least leave the last will? Truth be told, we know full well

the body's sprawled all black

Behold

the shattered soul of Mother Earth whose flesh is rotting off

The moment of death is walking up slowly

A poet, death in her arms, is walking dangerously over the paper.

LAND GRAB

Place a thumb on the dirt
ground, spread out and
swing
the other four fingers in
a cosmic arc, like ribs of
a fan,
now mine is the land
At the meager age ten
I was a vast landed
proprietor
with one whole town
under my thumb,
formidable to all
School playground and
our courtyard
sandy streamside
innocent alleys
where little kids' footfalls
like flowers come and go;
those patterns down on
earth
all the pretty imprints
upon the palms—where
have they sunk?

Grab it all the way to the
last bound under the wall
now it's just a matter of
climbing the wall, then
the flight through the sky,
I resolved to let my
unreachable mind soar up
and fluttered about the
sky to my heart's content,
that angel of imagination
was mine only;
those patterns up in
heavens
all the soaring wings—
where have they flown?

SHELTER

Let your body remember
Gusts of passion that hurl onto the edges of skies
your fingertips and another's
your navel and another's
your soul and another's—let your body remember all
Do not plunge
into that square magic box
where with just one click you can mingle with world's
wretches and rogues,
into the clutch of that rude contriving black hand
that holds sway of one whole world
Confer with the paper
on anything that interconnects your heart to another's
your eyes to another's
Upon that breath and body heat
will stir sensation back to life
then crystallize into a comforting inner shelter
with patterns natural and translucent.

THE EGGS OF ENVIRONMENTAL POLLUTION

On a day spring rain comes on soft feet
maybe it wants to rest awhile on tree-limbs
for the journey was so long—
drop by drop, those blooms of raindrops

Wish I could wreathe them round my neck
Angelic lips and tongue
cherubic iris
and tongue

How tempting,

I nearly popped one in my mouth
but oh no, don't
if you do you'll die
Don't put in your mouth
a drop of poison so pretty and black.

MUDFLAT

That black paper,
it's pregnant now

That paper crumpled blackish isn't a refuse
but a living mouth
licking earth's festering wounds;
a living lung
each of whose pores eliminates toxin from ailing men,
cradles vibrant, clean Nature;
earth's womb
bestowing all of self to those lives
engendering, bearing, then bearing anew and raising
filling men's open mouths again and again
with life

That black paper is
pregnant now.

LIFE

It happens only once
Never can be renewed
Don't call a crude scribble a practice
Don't whitewash a fault with the word 'experience'
Don't say mutual misunderstanding is an art

Already, the one leaf of paper's not to be used.

FORGIVING

Snow falls over Seorak Mountain
On every pine branch there's chaste nests
sheer white angel laughter cascades from the sky
That day I had my good fill of food, a bowl of hate
my face was aflame like a stove
my arrow, venom at the tip, aimed at a human being

Forgive
Forgive
Forgive
Why not awaken amid merciful snow
in Seorak Mountain far from the earthly for a while
Vacate the place where I sit

Don't even touch that paper.

SERENITY: MARSH

I think I know how deep it is

As I drift further and further from serenity
both feet mired in this generation's errors
that bind my hands and drags me off despite my
defiance

I rove through noises stumbling
for the place I want to reach
but handsome science cannot,
long lost are my ears
long lost are my eyes

Let alone my lost ears, my lost eyes
there's a place I want to be just as I am:
apparently all empty
and its depths unfathomable,
once I get there I'll be a sheet of paper.

AUTUMN SKY

God's paper it is

Glass paper made by
the very best craftsman

Everyplace seamless

Third-degree burns
from thunder-flames
gotten in a life time

have been healed
clean, no marks left

One steady gaze on
such paper,

I suppose, will smooth
out even crooked
scars.

CHARNEL HOUSE OF MANUSCRIPT PAPER

There were times when I wished to burrow into
a space of manuscript paper

But my daughters,

don't bury me in the wind

nor up in the sky

nor among trees

Grievous venoms spread throughout my body,

chafing wounds—saying *How sad, how sad*—
inflaming my heart,

don't leave their ashes behind

Burn off even my lingering attachment to a
single space of manuscript paper

and don't leave a spot in this world.

CHEEK

Someone

struck me

on the cheek,
whack!
A barrage of blows,
humiliation shot up flashing
fire through the sky
Somebody again hit me direct
in the heart burning red-hot
buzzing—on the taut surface of
this universe—and swelling up

The paper in its two arms
took in all of my life's red
marks and cradled.

EVEN IF I SLUMBER PILLOWED UPON A SWORD

The flesh at rest
the bones at rest
the tumult of fiery dances arrested
thunder, lightning, roaring billows calmed
my body's smarting pains briefly eased

into such paper I would meld

and become the paper

Even if I slumber pillowed upon a sword

in absolute quiet.

ABOUT THE AUTHOR

Shin Dal-Ja was born in Geochang, Gyongnam, in 1943. She studied at the Sookmyung Women's University and the Graduate School, where she received her doctorate. Winning the New Figure in Literature Award of the *Yeosang* in 1964 launched her literary career, then she made a subsequent debut in 1972, when Park Mok-Wol, a poet, commended her poems to the *Hyundae Munhak.*

She taught at the Pyungtaek University as a professor of Korean Literature, and later at Myungji College as a professor of Creative Writing. Her poetry books include *Consecrated Letters, The Songs of Solomon, Father's Light, While We Talk Long, Ardent Love,* and her essay collections *A Poet's Love, These Three Things Keep in Your Mind, At Forty I learned How to Walk through Life, Sorry-Thanks-Love You,* among many others. For her works she won the Literature of Korea Award, the Poetry and Poetics Award, the Poets' Association of Korea Award, the Modern Buddhist Literature Award, the Yongrang Poetry Award, and the Gongcho Literature Award.

COMMENTARY

POETICS THROUGH POEMS
KIM IN-WHAN (LITERARY CRITIC)

THE MAIN CONCERN IN READING A BOOK OF POEMS is to find the structural image linked to the overarching theme of the entire book. The construction of an entire piece of music is defined when one grasps the leitmotif of the piece; likewise, one can say one has read a book of poems only when he is enabled to contextualize each poem in light of this thematic image. *Paper* begins with the author declaring in her own 'note' the structural image, thus pretty much sparing the readers from pouring their endeavors themselves. Nonetheless, the book makes a singularly gripping read in that, even if one begins with a good knowledge of the theme, the placement of individual work is not within his easy reach.

The theme Shin wants to pursue in this poetry book is the image of paper. She represents objects and words in the same breath. Beginning with papyrus, clay, leaves, bamboo strips, silk, animal skin, she tracks the history of the invention of paper and its circulation, finally to affirm that the paper road is a spiritual path paved by the sacrifices of people like Chae Ryun, Go Sunji, Abbasid Caliph. Those who sacrificed for the cause are not heroes only. In the 16th century Netherlands, they made books out of the skin of slaves, prisoners, and executed criminals. There must have been some downright earnestness in the scholars who penned their poems on the skirt of Gisaeng, the ink imbuing every inch of her body. In Korean paper there is a sensation of midair that embraces everything world spews out. We expect to see very soon the paper made from kelp, such as seaweed. Shin likens the natural sensation of this paper, all chemicals removed, to naturalness, to somber and quiet temperament, to fresh and keen mind, of the Beloved. Thus she imagines in her mind a world cohabited by new men and new paper.

Shin's image of paper expands beyond her representation of objects. Life is written paper. On this paper people write, compose, and rewrite. As a matter of fact, there's a man who proved that life and letters are one. Jorges Luis Borges— he identified himself with books and served as a librarian and later the curator of the national library, lost sight and burrowed under darkness, traveling through letters to erect a castle of books. His books are still growing copious though his mind's eyes were sealed up forever. Borges' books signify to Shin the very paper which carries writings like mother's milk that satisfies an infant's hunger. Furthermore, she perceives the world as an enormous library, and nature an enormous paper. Autumn sky is God's paper; summer leaves dark green paper whose darkness expels brushes; waves blue paper that manages to rise up no matter how much it is crumpled. Shin is given snow, which is no earthly black paper but pure silver paper, something forbidden to the implacable. She sees in a magnolia blossom the paper she'd love to bury a line of her life poem, feels in autumn field the still of a leaf of paper that has grown immensely sensitive. She translates the pond in Yulmae, a village in Sancheong, into a signature on the scroll picture of Mt. Jiri. Mudflat, reeds, marsh, black swan, great swan, yellow spoon bird, black-headed seagull—all these are letters for her to read. Hers has been a life brimming with an appetence to respond wholeheartedly to nature's faintest call. Innumerable poets before her have taken the same path; Shin, however, considers it her own task to always travel into unknown land. For poetry should not be tethered to the bedpost of deductive logic. A poet, through his mind's eyes, must illuminate nature's letters all over, and reread them anew. A poet who has not discovered how to best illuminate letters suffers the unease, while trying to find his place. This unease presses him on to wage war against himself, urging that he find his authentic place. Every poet needs an empty spot from which he can go elsewhere in search of self. In her poem titled 'Furrow' Shin calls that spot a canyon where she'd like to erect a temple. The furrow in a surrendered person's face is like a canyon. The temple erected there is not swept away in water or wind.

In real life, somehow, there's no room for empty spots as we think in terms of rules and numerical values, ending up succumbing to statistics. Here we are governed by technology, and questions that can only be answered with 'yes' or 'no' are considered legitimate. Individuals live on mistaking themselves for their own cards. A communication in which one delivers and the other receives messages by means of a tool cannot be called, in strict sense, a communication. Something fundamental is lacking in the relationship between one tool and the other. One's listening to the other, but cannot understand the other. That is an unprocessed exchange, a deal devoid of mutual communication. Think about wares, for whose exchanges you have a marketplace. You take money and get what you need, so then the deal is done. Nobody wants any further relationship. Shin believes that paper can be a charm in mercantile society where exchange value works as absolute value.

If you tire out, all giddy
flustered navigating

from site to site,
then take a sheet of blank paper
and with all your mind
write down each letter of your name
stroke by stroke.

—from "Charm"

Shin doesn't believe "that square magic box / where with just one click you can mingle with world's wretches and rogues" ("Shelter"). Hence her conviction: not a door whose secret code, or your fingerprint or voice can open, but one that welcomes you with a mortal voice and mortal hands, or better yet, some fond brushwood door "that comes down only to your knees, left open day and night ("Analogue") provides a better way for men to live humanly. She then presents her objection to the splendid civilization that takes over every nook and cranny and mar human nature. Poetry is "like paper, the last comfort for the broken-hearted ("Island"); its task is to forge an island away from the control of techniques. When we succumb to the latter the wellspring of life is depleted. Instrumentalism turns a man untrue to his own existence. A person unable to admire is a torpid, tired being. Shin finds a long-sought leaf of paper from God in the Amish who inhabit the region of Lancaster, Pennsylvania, forgoing cars, electricity, water pipes or school. She wants to keep the town as it is. "My body grew so light, nearly translucent, that I soared up and up; couldn't even put a period, everything turning translucent upon that pristine, vivid paper / I didn't bring back even a single sheet of it, I left all behind; / left all my footmarks even..." ("The Amish"). Shin's heroine is Julia Butterfly Hill, who lived in a tree almost two years, fighting against the lumber company scheduled to exploit the redwood forest in North California. "You are Woman of all women. A heroine at 24" ("Human Butterfly"). Shin tastes life's flavor and attempts to share it with others. Technology that repeats itself in the manner of a recorder deprives men of the ability to savor this flavor. To be loyal to self, one must have mental courage enough to deliver oneself from tedious batches of duties. Those who violate restraints of mercantile society end up paying the price of sacrilege. Poetic intuition holds a demand for values that are never universal. And these values have lost trust in mercantile society. An iron will only can esteem values ignored by all. Shin presents objections to the broken world seemingly in good order but without heartbeat. A worldly man in mercantile society is unable to meet urgent demands of life. He does not grasp the space necessary between himself and his object.

The first object emerging in Shin's self-search is the past as the present, to wit, her memories. The mind's bright eyes capture bits of recollection before they sink away, then revivify all those direct and unique experiences. Irreconcilable directness of life turns Shin to things the most intimate to her. She tells us what it is like to be deprived of recollection's directness, and that life should not be this way. One can provide false information in one's résumé but cannot write down falsehood in regards to one's recollection. Shin upholds the truth of her recollection, fights against self, brings to life private experiences indefinable by voluntary memory. Proust declares that the pathway to the true experience of things past is not by volition and contemplation but by involuntary memory. On this pathway paved with indescribable humiliation and misery, Shin experiences the absolute convergence of the past and future. To her the lost paradise is the sole paradise. No one else but exiles come to learn the true meaning of the homeland. Shin's matrix is nostalgia. Her home, no matter how far away she is at the moment, remains the center of her being. The stellar adolescence as the girl gathered stars to fix rice and gimchi with; jumbled writing along with clumsy drawing of an unseen train on the walls of her childhood home; countless letters she wrote over rice and sawdust, in the snow and sod, on the sand as well as her older brother's grave; paper boats she folded and floated to an unknown world every night; the wings she begged for so that she could grab the sky after grabbing with her small hands all the land in the village—all these worked together to bring a poet out of a country girl.

>

As a young girl
I once felt like a bit of soft flesh fall off my crotch
Mother said
You see, it's your first flowers
I thought hard but it didn't seem like flowers
so I locked the door, dabbed the thing on the paper;
was no flesh, nor red blood,
nor anything like flowers
A fatal memorandum
portending the foray of the one
who offered up to paper her first menstruation
her virginity

and thus had intimacy with the paper,
from whence she will not part ever.

—"Mother Said, Your First Flowers"

Shin gave paper her first cycle and remembers it as adultery with it. Baudelaire says that writing poetry is an act of prostitution, and sure enough, anything below par cannot be poetry; it isn't hard to understand that to be a poet in a mercantile society is, more often than not, considered an accursed thing. One cannot be a poet unless one accepts certain grievances, certain unfairness. Devotion to poetry involves voluntary sacrifice of one's success in a mercantile society. Being a poet is neither glory nor misery to the poet. It's just fate. At twenty Shin roved for a stave she had written down on the ground with a twig, and such pattern continued all through her life. Not forgetting the old resolution to confront a sheet of paper, which gave her a cut on the lip, she reaffirms her will to fiercely absorb herself with paper, gladly risking another cut. She knows nothing else to depend on, for paper is the only thing that accepts all sorts of humiliation in life. Her life of 70 years, four seasons, America and France and Asia, compassion and shame and rapture and betrayal, her lover's soul, the future yet to be traveled —she loaded them all in the paper, only to find the bottom space hardly filled. A million birds, a million tons of rocks, the sea and fishes in it, all of the villagers, charge that she bring them back to life from their silent confinement.

A human being cannot disjoin himself from the others. What reforms a poet internally is the others. Self-search is impossible without the latter. In each man's core lies communal core, and his subjectivity is mutual. When a poet speaks of himself his words purport to inform others of himself. What is really vital to us is togetherness. The one person that was with you at your birth scene is your mother. Shin recalls white, fleshy, large hips of her mother as the latter passed water, unlikely to shatter. Mother's tears were the young poet's hoops, fivestones and beanbags. Not until years later did she realize they were indeed mother's flesh and heart. Some time after their debt-ridden house passed into the possession of someone else, Shin's mother attempted suicide but failed, studied Korean language late in her life and sent a note to her daughter: "Dont foget what I say, Study til you die, Make monney, Dont live like me, Be happey" ("Coughing up Blood"). A lump of maternal blood poured on the paper sustained Shin all along. Her father, who loved women and songs and padduk, went bankrupt and gave up songs and command of his life, then experienced a new birth and died as a man of honest essence.

We live in a time when the word 'together' is losing its meaning. In a world where people take simple kindness and close relationship unfeasible and untrustworthy, articles worn-out and not to be trusted, a guest is diminished to a mere customer and good will toward the hurt is seen as ineffectual interference. All of us have become powermongers desirous of flaunting success in today's mercantile society deprived of harmonious rhythm, which is innate in men of good will. Shin would love to see the gourd that her grandmother sewed up for further use, misses big lumps on those common men and women. Evil is akin to the form of war where the invalid are trampled. Insofar as evil exists, goodness should be taken as a form of war rather than a form of peace. Goodness is associated with brotherly love treating weaker ones and losers with civility. Shin sees a man "vested with a sheet of paper, crossing the abysmal heart of winter" ("Paper Comforter").

> lying down in the wintry subway passage,
> a sheet of paper sheltering him from
> the world's winds
> a sheet of paper holding all of his past years
>
> –from "Paper Comforter"

Shin portrays this man as "a dubious, obscure mark." In old times when men did have hearts they called a beggar a passer-by. Shin feels that the thread connecting one person to another has come loose, though she makes no mention of it here.

Division is a realistic experience to those who still carry nostalgia of unification. The kind of hope one gains by disregarding painful truths is mere deception.

Ideological interests and suchlike fundamentally do not matter to Shin. She can only note how her own body reacts and then give us analytical report. At the inception of analysis, however, poetry departs from corporal reality to merge into reproductive medium, that is, language. In whatever case, the body cannot be the instrument. We are not capable of distinguishing what we feel from what our bodies feel, and what we feel of ourselves from what we feel of another object. Feelings do not occur to us by physical means.

for the place I want to reach
but handsome science cannot

–from "Serenity: Marsh"

The body is not an object but a subject. Even a slave cannot shake off the feeling that his body belongs to him, not to his master. We are unable to understand the body objectively because the body cannot be translated into the language of the object. Poetry is a task to delve into the internal circumstance which cannot be revived. "The very instant / a man's heart touches the paper's heart" ("The Soul of Art") poetry is forged. The dynamics between a poet and poetry works the same way as does the dynamics between a farmer and his sod. It is a superficial view to affirm that the latter's anguish is tantamount to effectiveness or profitability. Sod is a mystery beyond the farmer's volition and intelligence. Shin wagers the whole of her being to assail the core of life and thence accepts the world. To accept is to welcome. Acceptance spells hospitality. To respond is like to be responded. To respond with our whole being is reckoned as contemplation. Contemplation is not viewing. The viewer, out of curiosity without misgivings, can only scratch the surface of matters. He does not apply himself to what's taking place at the moment. There is no curiosity for future in contemplating reality. The very moment viewing translates into contemplation, the meaning alters and poetry is forged. Shin dubs poetry Paper Porridge.

Remove from the world's proverbs any imperfection
let your spiritual silence and contemplation
be so very pure
exercise patience abiding
now is born a balmy Word,
O world!
I will apply it to your sore

—from "Paper Porridge"

External knowledge and internal contemplation work in contradiction. A contemplator holds quiet about himself, withdraws from the object, then enters into reality. To withdraw from the object is not to abrogate reality, but to keep the way it is. Shin falls prostrate "on her face // flat on the ground // mouth sealed, ears open // then ears closed, eyes open // to creep" ("A Sacred Place") and "death in her arms, is walking dangerously over the paper" ("Death"). As there's no intrinsic answer we remain inexplicable to ourselves. Self-search is an impossible goal. For one is bound to misconceive one's own self. Life, to anyone, is a pilgrimage that cannot be immobilized. Immobility is a fantasy, a delusion, to all humanity. Shin, therefore, is obliged to have the fortitude of a desert-walker.

Desert road, where you walk all day long only to see later the same traces already effaced by winds, is a trackless road. "Plodding, hobbling over that desert" ("Blank Paper 3), Shin now has to show forth "all the fingerprint of the sand-blown desert" (Hand Printing). There in the desert, she cables in words the paper's soul. That paper is an infinite stretch of barren soil; you "put your whole life to plow" it, yet "still cannot till even a single parcel" (Tilling of Mind).

CHO YOUNG-SHIL is the translator of four Korean poetry collections: *One Day, Then Another* by Kim Kwang-Kyu (White Pine Press, 2013), *A Warm Family* by Kim Hu-Ran (Codhill Press, 2014), *A Lion at Three in the Morning* by Nam Jin-Woo (Homa & Sekey Books, 2017), and *Whisper of Splendor* by Chong Hyon-Jong (Homa & Sekey Books, 2018).

She wrote a book of poems in memoriam of her mother (1908-2001), and in her spare time writes poems for young adults and translates children's picture books from Korean into English.